AUGUST MOON

By

Shawn Powell

© 2003 by Shawn Powell. All rights reserved.

No part of this book may be reproduced, stored in a retrieval system, or transmitted by any means, electronic, mechanical, photocopying, recording, or otherwise, without written permission from the author.

ISBN: 1-4107-5723-4 (e-book)
ISBN: 1-4107-5722-6 (Paperback)

Library of Congress Control Number: 2003093461

This book is printed on acid free paper.

Printed in the United States of America
Bloomington, IN

1stBooks - rev. 08/20/03

To my children: Alayna Nicole,

Derek Xavier and Autumn Jacquelyn

In precious memory of my Grandfather Jack Fite, My Grandmother Mary Powell, my Aunt Maudie Eddington and my good friend George Bradley

CREDITS

Book Cover
- *Zheng Li, artist*
- *Lee Brothers Studio Gallery*
- *Roswell, GA*

Title of Artwork: Season. No. 1

Back Cover
- *Jorge Alvarez, photographer*
- *Erin Dougherty, assistant photographer*
- *Jorge Alvarez Studio*
- *Tampa, FL*

Photographs
- *Submitted by Rita Kallal*

ACKNOWLEDGMENTS

It is said, that God will never burden a soul with more hardship than that person can possibly handle. During the days in which my spirit lagged and the sunken path that I trudged through seemed more endless with each step, I questioned God's presence while desperately searching for a helping hand or a kind word of encouragement. It is only now that I realize the importance of those whom I have bared my soul to over the years. These people have given me strength and hope through times of heartache, pain and triumph.

To Kerry Meyers, Greg Spratt and Sam Cox...thank you for always being there for me. You have never turned away from me when I was in need. You have never judged me. You have always taken a genuine interest in my life and the life of my children and I thank you from the bottom of my heart.

To Mark Littlefield, Mike Garrett, David Robinson, John Szponar, Terry Rupp, Lou Maggio, Hal Steinbrenner, Ian Rubel, David and Kim Gephart and the Keith Pickett family thank you for lending an ear and a helping hand when I was searching for answers. You are true friends and I am truly blessed to have you in my life.

To Maggie Pickett, Elise Wendell, Linda Gardner and Robin Swartz...thank you for your inspiration.

To the family members and friends that touched my life so much that their memories thrive within my writings...thank you.

To Mike Unger and Brian Simmons, thank you for your technical support and your friendship.

To Jorge Alvarez and Erin Dougherty thank you for your generosity and friendship.

Thank you God, for your guiding light. Thank you for bringing these special people into my life, Your presence shines through them all.

INTRODUCTION

Life is a series of peaks and valleys. Sometimes, when you feel you are standing on top of the world, it is at that point you realize the ground below is rising around the mountain top in which you stand. You realize the once lofty perch that protected you from the struggles of life is now mired in a bog of pain and suffering. You struggle to escape the quicksand, but the strength you possess is not enough to lift yourself free. At this point in time, you realize the importance of friends, family and faith in God.

Through the fires of my life, I have become a stronger person. With this book, I share with you my most inner-personal struggles, my deepest thoughts and more than all, my soul. My eternal prayer is for harmony. A solemn peace that will allow me to grow as a human, so I might become a better father, a better son, a better friend and a better person on this earth.

My path will continue up steep mountain sides and down through treacherous crevasses, but with each step I take, I know God is looking over me...

May the simple words of August Moon warm your heart and bring a smile to your face.

AUGUST MOON

STORY POEM I

Shawn Powell

THE MANGO TREE

Within the land of Sugar Cane,
the island's heat did swoon;
I sat upon a Palm tree stump,
the time was nearly noon.

I gazed upon a playing field,
where boys revealed their game;
Upon a diamond in the rough,
Bad hops displayed no shame.

The sun was bearing straight for me,
My collar soaked in sweat;
I reached inside my travel bag,
In search of something wet.

My throat was dry, the dust was thick
as it twirled across the field;
I longed to quench my dreadful thirst,
But, no beverage would I yield.

Shawn Powell

As I slowly raised my eyes ahead,
I spied a boy of ten;
Who stood in tattered shoes of gray,
His body frail and thin.

His shorts were brown much like his
skin, his T-shirt had been torn;
He knew no other life on earth,
impoverished he was born.

He glared at me with cautious eyes,
As my tote remained unzipped;
On top there lay a pack of gum,
inside his heart had flipped.

I took the gum out of the bag,
and offered him the pack;
But with one finger, bony thin,
he signaled "I'll be back".

And as he darted across the road,
I watched him pick up speed;
He jumped a fence, he showed no sense,
He climbed a Mango Tree.

In record time he scaled the trunk,
then returned back to the ground;
Over the road, he burned a path;
He raced the speed of sound.

I stood amazed, this boy had solved,
the problem to my thirst;
With fruit in hand it swelled with juice;
He answered my need first.

As I handed him the pack of gum,
I saw his bleeding hand;
His smile dimmed the brightest star,
as he stood in burning sand.

And I pondered why a boy of ten,
would risk his life for me;
When so-called friends would hide away,
if problems they would see.

As I sat upon that tree stump,
The boy soon drifted free;
And I found a friend for life that day,
He climbed the Mango Tree.

Shawn Powell

CHAPTER ONE
SPIRITUAL INSPIRATION

Shawn Powell

WITHOUT FAITH, THERE IS NO AIR TO BREATHE;
NO WATER TO QUENCH THE SOUL WHEN IT IS THIRSTY;
WITHOUT FAITH, LUNGS ARE FILLED WITH DUST OF THE EARTH,
AND THE DESICCATED FOUNTAINS ARE FOREVER VOID OF NOURISHMENT;
WITHOUT FAITH, WE CANNOT LIVE.
WITHOUT FAITH, WE CANNOT DIE.

AUGUST MOON

On a clear, warm night in August past,
an ardent moon did gleam;
High above the clouds its sailed,
The sky was like its stream.

Below the orb, I stood in awe,
betwixt the forest trees;
Pearl Blue streaks enticing life,
within celestial breeze.

I watched as beauty glistened forth,
in radiant allure;
Inside a circle of my mind; All separate
thoughts were pure.

My first thought concentrated on the
brilliance of each ray;
That danced upon each veiny leaf and
beckoned one to play.

Shawn Powell

To touch each sparkle that appeared;
New energy abound;
To lavish in the moonlit night,
A child's heart was found

A second thought revealed a soul,
that hungered for its song;
Exposed within a melody,
the cadence surging strong

The third and fourth thoughts differed
much from those that came before;
Thoughts so deep and well refined,
childish thoughts no more.

Light propelled in mystic flame,
sorted mindful thought;
Bringing hope that present life
was worthy, not for naught.

I looked upon the life I led,
I questioned every turn;
I wondered how my life might be;
My choices caused concern.

But, as the light from up above
filtered down to me;
I realized, the life I knew
was truly meant to be.

For God had planned a life for me,
My problems he would mend;
His love restored my loathsome heart,
He freed me from my sin.

I recognized when times were bleak,
the skies appeared pitch black;
But each time I was knocked around,
I always bounced right back.

And though at times, no light was sent,
from the source which reigned on high;
The ray of hope that dwelled within,
kept me, from asking Why?

And on this night in August past,
an ardent moon did sail;
And I found my peace, for now I knew,
God's light would never fail.

Shawn Powell

ALL WORRIES, WE HAVE NONE

Swirling Clouds, in constant change,
Hypnotic to our sight;
On Backs we lie, on Summer days
and watch as birds take flight.

As children on this Mighty Earth
we long for changing skies;
From Baby Blue to Midnight Grey,
we pause with open eyes.

We anticipate with wonderment,
as Darkness raids the sun;
We hide in shelter of a tree;
'Til the storm cloud's wrath is done

But now and then, in pouring rain
we drop our fear and run;
Beneath the grisly skies above,
All Worries, We Have None.

AUGUST MOON

Our spirits cleansed though body soiled;
Our soul now hints the urge;
To beckon forth the burning light,
so anxious to emerge.

And as the sun is called to warm
the hearts of all who live;
It lurks behind a darkened wall,
Its life it wants to give.

And all the children know in time
the sun will shine once more;
And deliver life through colors bright,
a prism to adore.

The changing sky gives hope and faith;
that all days are not one;
The changing sky makes children muse;
All Worries, We Have None.

The smiles of the changing sky
soon disappear with age;
In time the sky, was but forgot,
or blamed in utter rage.

Shawn Powell

We can't remember smiling, when
cool raindrops splashed our face;
With open mouth, we caught the drops;
As we twirled inside our space

Now we speed about our lives,
Our laughter rings no more;
We forget about the logic found;
What the lamp of day was for.

The changing sky, no more our friend;
We failed to keep the sun;
Our hearts are dead; There's no more rain;
All Worries, We Have None

THE TURNING SAND

On sands of white, I strolled in thought
as waves crashed to the shore;
Reflections of my life unveiled,
inside each charging roar.

The sand of old, is laid to rest,
in the grayish plots of past;
Soaking up the sun's bright blaze;
Its days are fading fast.

In present time, the sand is tan
and lives within each ebb;
In constant change it looks for peace,
within a sea-green web.

Concealed within the ocean's depths,
All life begins anew;
The birth of sand in neutral shade,
below a mist of blue.

Shawn Powell

The journey of the sand begins,
deep in the seabed's womb;
And sadly ends in pale-white scorn,
Amidst a dusty tomb.

I watched that day upon a rock,
that jutted towards the sea;
And saw myself; A grain of sand,
that someday would be free.

SILHOUETTE

Along the darkened journey, down the twisting roads of night
we bump into so many faces, one and then another;
Often times we do not stop to ask them of their names
we speed through our existence, we look beyond their worlds;
Burdened with our problems, we fail to see the pain that fills
a desperate person that searches for a smile;
A pleasant word, or just hello from the lips of one who cares,
A notice from another, gives meaning to their life;
We are so blind as humans to pass strangers in the sun,
Just silhouettes of faces and outlines of our mirrored self;
Only a handful of people in this world, have the gift to infuse
life into the soul of those who are in dire need of kindness;
Only a handful of people in this world, have made a difference
amongst our peers, by sharing a smile or a hug;
Along my darkened journey, down the twisting roads of night,
your smile has given sunlight to my existence…
And life unto the silhouette of whom I've always been.

Shawn Powell

WHAT IF?

What if the world was not a sphere,
that turned to meet the sun?
What if the skies were void of rain,
and rivers could not run?

Life would have no merit,
We'd hide in constant fear;
"What if" controls our future,
for decisions are unclear.

Tucked away in shadows,
we hide upon a shelf;
A compromised position
that transforms one's inner self.

A shelf so high, you can't look down
for fear that you will fall;
A shelf so narrow in its base,
you cling unto the wall.

AUGUST MOON

The choices of our daily life,
will change without a doubt;
But living with a fear of trust,
Is not what life's about.

Do not shun the road ahead,
your life is God's great gift;
And if you hide upon the shelf,
you'll only know "What If".

Shawn Powell

SKIPPING STONES

Upon the bank of a tranquil pond,
amongst the woodland trees;
I gathered flat and shiny rocks,
as twigs dug in my knees.

I piled all the stones I found,
their shapes, not one the same;
With grimy hands I took my stand,
and started up my game.

This game was very simple,
quite primitive in fact;
The object was to skip each stone
across the water's tract.

And hopefully a side-arm fling
would make it's way across;
And land upon the other side,
ten skips from just one toss.

Then the victory would be mine,
I'd shout for all to hear;
For this task is not as simple,
as the image would appear.

This game had now begun for me,
The goal was now in sight;
Could I reach the other side?
I'd try with all my might.

At first I'd throw the stone too hard,
and to the bottom it would sink;
Then the stone would sail awry,
and vanish in a blink.

I tried and tried to get it right,
to skip the stone across;
But only six or seven skips,
would make it with each toss.

But as the evenings shade encroached,
upon the woodland trees;
I selected one last stone to throw,
against the steadfast breeze.

Shawn Powell

I often think about the days,
when goals were just a game;
Attainable through sweat and tears,
to fail, revealed no shame.

Goals are set to prod us on,
to fulfill each dream within;
Without these goals we'd waste away,
A sloth, we'd be akin.

So take the stone unto your hand,
and with fervor let it fly;
For the goals you set are not so tough,
if only you would try.

For when I threw that final stone,
amongst the woodland trees;
My dream became reality,
ten skips were but a breeze.

THE PATH

I stared inside a twirling trance,
as the world I've known untwists;
Untangling webs of yesteryear,
My struggling mind persists

Subjective choices were conveyed,
Yet no answer could I find;
Shrouded within the catacombs,
of a child's simple mind

What was the force that held me
back from the road that lay ahead;
Did I fear the great unknown?
Or was my route misled?

I assume there was some logic,
in the footmarks that I made;
But the trail was so ambiguous,
At times, my trust would fade.

Shawn Powell

Would my love be grander with the
one I longed to kiss;
Would my passion fulminate,
Would she bathe in splendid bliss.

How would my children differ; Would
they be much like they are?
Would they still blaze through the midnight sky,
much like a shooting star.

I think of how life could have been,
had I served the other choice;
But, inner strength expanded when
I'd heed my inner voice.

My prayer is for tranquility, to accept
the changes of each day;
I pray for courage with each step,
God's wisdom leads my way.

For the imprints made upon the path
that I chose so long ago;
Have grown in faith, without regret,
So Onward I must go.

CARRY ME

If I could look down from above,
and chart my lifelong walk;
I'd find a map of peaks and valleys,
lined with blood and chalk.

On the map of life each step I traced,
revealed a rough terrain;
And often times the road was long,
and overwrought with pain.

I carried burdens every day,
upon this darkened road;
I stumbled many times it seemed,
collapsing with each load.

When I'd fall, I'd cry out loud,
I'd scream without control;
My pain was great, I doubted Faith,
for trouble filled my soul.

Shawn Powell

On my knees, I would remain,
upon the stony plane;
Until I felt my strength return;
My trust I'd soon regain.

I'd scale the rocky, mountain base
as sweat would burn my eyes;
I'd wipe it clean, and climb some more,
despite my trembling thighs.

As I climbed the lofty ridges,
my agile feet did soar;
Atop the sturdy mountain peak,
where burdens lived no more.

But as I occupied the mount,
A figure walked below;
This person took the very path,
I trod so long ago.

He carried weight upon his back
how much? I could not tell;
His body slumped upon each stride,
In silence he would dwell.

He shuffled 'neath the crushing mass,
while blisters warped his feet;
He trudged the lonesome sandstone,
as he labored through the heat.

Then up the mountain he'd ascend,
though He could not wipe his eyes;
With bonded hands, his face was hid,
in a crimson-red disguise.

As he climbed on to the rocky crest,
to the place in which I stood;
I caught a glimpse of this weary man,
and then I understood.

A rugged cross aligned his back, his
hands were strapped in lace;
A crown of thorns adorned his head,
as blood poured down his face.

Without words He spoke to me,
So my eyes could clearly see;
The very man, who walked my path,
be nailed upon the tree.

Shawn Powell

Jesus sacrificed his life, for He
loves us all the same;
He carries us upon his back;
Our Everlasting Flame.

He could have called ten thousand Angels,
But then where would we be?
Instead he carried all our sins,
when he died on Calvary.

So when you walk upon your path,
Life's heartaches will occur;
But, the greatest blessing of our Lord,
one day we'll all incur.

And on the day, your name is
called and you are glory bound;
Once again He'll carry you,
Though his footsteps make no sound.

ANGEL ON CALL

All children born unto this world,
From blackness into light;
With bleary eyes, they cannot tell
the day from dark of night.

As children grow ideas are formed,
they're guided by their source;
They learn about both life and love,
They're set upon their course.

As years build on, they sail their sea,
testing waters deep;
Dreams of who they long to be,
invade them during sleep.

They venture out, sometimes too far,
they stumble in defeat;
But strength instilled from unchanged love,
returns them to their feet.

And through the grave and dismal days,
there will be but ONE;
Whose soul was sent to mend their pain,
No matter what's been done.

And in the child's darkest days,
when faith has lost its charm;
An Angel's hand will calm their fear,
and promise no more harm.

A loving touch that quenches dread,
will roam within the child;
Revealing gifts from God above,
new confidence brims wild.

A lifted spirit dwells within,
the body fills with pride;
The Angel pulls the child up,
and brings her to his side.

No more a child in this world,
A woman now is found;
She finds the secret of her heart;
Her cries have no more sound.

AUGUST MOON

When her life's beneath the shadow,
her human side may fall;
But her smile will return again,
Her Angel is on Call.

Shawn Powell

LIFE

The most trying time in a person's
life is their entrance to this world;
The body torques, the trauma builds,
as shapes becomes unfurled.

Into a blinding light we come,
our minds completely white;
Dependent on a caring touch,
we undertake each plight.

Life gets tougher as we grow,
decisions bear much weight;
Often times we fall face first,
when the weight becomes too great.

Depression fills the void of loss,
a crumbling mind in pain;
We search for stillness in our head,
to relieve the inward strain.

With stinging tears, and a crying voice,
we struggle for a clue;
Why oh why, My Lord oh why,
Whatever did I do?

Within this suffering we've indulged,
Our eyes do not see true;
For the many blessings we receive,
have failed to come in view

But, once we step into the light
to the touch of his caring hands;
God will ease our agony, our
prayers he understands.

Life is a journey, come what may,
we fall, for we are men;
But our blessings best each sorrow,
and our sun will rise again.

Shawn Powell

IN THE PALM OF HIS HAND

In the palm of his hand, he wielded
terror, relentless shards of doom;
An assault of evil tidings, causing
Never ending gloom.

In the palm of her hand, lay the salty
tears, a mighty country grieves;
Yet her glory still shines eminent,
Standing tall as passion weaves.

In the palm of his hand, lay a fireman's
wrist, with a pulse that beats no more;
The priest implores God's mercy,
Now he walks the Golden Shore.

In the palm of his hand, lays sifted rubble
stained with innocent blood;
He clinches up his aching hands,
with a tear-streaked face of mud.

In the palm of her hand, lays a photograph,
of a loved one she can't trace;
The picture wilts with every tear that
splashes on his face.

In the palm of His Hand, He mends the
wings of the angels he has blessed;
He takes them home to be with him,
Where they will find true rest.

In the palm of His hand, lay the scars
of hope, received so long ago;
Raindrops lace the morning sky,
Through His tears, our hearts shall grow.

Shawn Powell

STORY POEM II

Shawn Powell

YONDER IS THE DONKEY

When I was just a shaver,
my years were probably five;
I rode inside my Grandpa's Ford,
as we motored up his drive.

A treacherous lane that dipped through trees,
and climbed up hills so steep;
We bounced along our merry way,
His truck much like a jeep.

As we reached the driveways' apex,
Through the window he would point;
I pressed my face up to the glass,
and followed his crooked joint.

Out upon a rolling dale, amid
the bluegrass lea;
Tucked inside its velvet green,
as far as eyes could see.

Shawn Powell

Cattle draped the hillsides,
Angus black and Hereford red;
There must have been a thousand
grazing bovine being fed.

Along the weed-filled roadside,
foxtails lined the fence;
He parked his rusted truck there,
amongst the thistles dense.

He took me from the front seat,
and stood me in the bed;
He searched the pasture down below,
then his hat leapt from his head.

"Yonder is the Donkey, do you see
him in the herd?;"
But all my straining eyes could find,
were some cattle and a bird.

Finally in the massive group,
his gray ears, I would find;
So different from the others,
but the donkey didn't mind.

AUGUST MOON

Sometimes the Donkey ventured up to
the fence where we would stand;
I fed him apples and carrot sticks, as
he'd eat them from my hand.

This trend lived on for many years
as my sisters' joined the quest;
We'd comb the green, green pasture
'til the sun would find its rest.

Over the great horizon, the fiery
sun would fade;
Much like the interest in my friend;
future visits seldom made

On the last day that I saw the farm,
I made one final stop;
Along the very roadside, where the
foxtails bloomed atop.

As I searched the hilly meadow,
for two ears so tall and gray;
The Ole' Gray Donkey hid from me,
as the crickets chirped away

Shawn Powell

My Grandpa pulled up next to me,
and said "He is not here;
He passed away this winter, the harsh
conditions too severe."

It's funny, how we all presume,
each day is like before;
Yonder is the Donkey, yet we see
him, nevermore.

CHAPTER TWO
COPING WITH LOSS

Shawn Powell

Like jagged blades into my flesh, the piercing howls
exalt their whims of pain;
And I weep into my hands for my tears know not
where to empty;
But with each salty teardrop that weighs upon my
dampened lashes;
I become stronger and I realize, they are not gone…
They live within each breath I take.

THE MIGHTY SHIP

One restless night, I sat in bed,
as night controlled the sky;
Hopeless thoughts repressed my
sleep, no matter what I'd try.

I could not seem to shut my eyes,
for sadness ruled my mind;
But as I finally drifted off,
Relief is what I'd find.

For I dreamed that night of a Mighty Ship,
docked along the bay;
Construction was magnificent,
In current, it would sway.

Upon the bow of this Mighty Ship,
a Captain manned the wheel;
Releasing ties that held the ship,
into a sea of teal.

Shawn Powell

The ship was launched, upon its way,
Life's journey had begun;
Crashing waves would drench the stern,
As the ship sailed t'wards the sun.

The ship would stop from time to time,
as children came aboard;
Scared, they huddled down below;
Above, the ocean roared.

Onward ho, the vessel sailed
as swells would climb its path;
But steady was this ship in war,
it battled nature's wrath.

Through raging seas, and waters calm,
Life's journey was complete,
The Mighty Ship had met each crest,
With the power of a fleet.

And when the Mighty Ship had docked,
along the barren shore;
The passengers emerged unscathed;
But the ship could sail no more.

For the ship had found its calming lull,
upon the tranquil sand.
And those who sailed within its guard,
soon learned to understand.

The vessel's strength provided
life to all who dwelled within;
A course was set and then achieved,
A protector he had been.

This mighty ship, it laid in rest,
Its life no longer found;
A consoling rush of soothing tide,
remained the only sound.

Awakened by each vision seen;
My eyes soon dried of tears;
I saw the life of one so close,
The dream had calmed my fears.

As people live, they too must die,
As sad as this may be;
But the memory of their living soul,
Means more than life to me.

Shawn Powell

And as I peered outside my room,
into the star-filled night;
I looked upon one lucky star,
that burned the sky so bright.

I realized, from that point on,
How lucky I must be;
To know I had a Mighty Ship
that brought me through the sea.

So as I gaze through black of night,
unto the twinkling sky;
I give to you my Grandpa dear,
This loving wish Goodbye.

ARMS OF LOVE

In the arms of a loving mother,
lies a newborn, soft and weak;
The mother cradles this Gift from
God, as tears race down her cheek.

She holds this precious lil' girl,
and whispers of her love;
Her eyes well up, her breath is short,
as she stares from up above.

She promises to take care of her,
and never leave her side;
She will always be her guiding light,
Her smile gleamed with pride.

As the baby grew into a child, and
the child into a teen,
The mother took her everywhere,
Her watchful eye so keen.

Shawn Powell

Through illness and through heartache,
the Mother's hand was there;
To pull her lil' girl from pain, and
relieve her from despair.

One day, upon life's winding road,
An illness came to be;
And the pillar of strength the lil' girl
knew was crashing to the sea.

The lil' girl's world was upside down,
Her guiding light drew pale;
But, the Mother kept her promises, and
refused to ever fail.

Then one day, the Mother's pain,
was too unbearable to withstand;
So the lil' girl approached her mom,
and took her by the hand.

She told her Mother, she'd be all right
though she lied with every breath;
She wanted to release her pain, but
could not accept her death.

AUGUST MOON

In the arms of a loving daughter,
lay her Mother soft and weak;
The daughter cradles this Gift from God,
as tears raced down her cheek.

She held this precious woman,
and whispered of her love;
Her eyes welled up, her breath was short
as she stared from up above.

For she held her Mother in her arms
as she breathed her final sighs;
Quietly, She drifts away,
but Her promise never dies.

Shawn Powell

ONE MORE DAY

Give her one more day,
My Lord,
Give her one more day.

Let her sing one lullaby,
as she rocks me fast asleep;
Let her fingers graze my face,
to calm me as I weep.

Let her brush my hair once more,
Let her tie my shoes;
Let her steal away my tears,
and kiss away each bruise.

Give her one more day,
My Lord,
Give her one more day.

Let her argue yes or no,
Let her raise her voice;
Let her tell me what to do,
and I will serve her choice.

I do not want to see her go,
Give me one more day;
Who will be there in her stead,
to wipe these tears away.

Give me one more day,
My Lord,
Give me one more day.

Let her stay with me my Lord,
upon my knees I pray;
Why did she have to leave my world?
Please give me one more day.

Trust in God, He hears your prayer,
For He will grant your plea;
But He'll not give just one more day,
He'll give eternity.

Shawn Powell

PEACE OF THE HEART

The time is now, the waiting game
has come unto an end;
I must retrieve the heart I gave
For now my life must mend.

I sacrificed my soul and mind
to secure my perfect mate;
But now I've come to understand
My bleeding soul must wait.

Picking up the pieces of a
puzzle too involved;
I cannot face more torture,
My turmoil needs resolved.

I dreamed one night, that God above,
Had taken my weary hand;
He wiped away the tears I'd shed,
He seemed to understand.

He raised me up and showed me,
all my needs were being met;
And yes they were, All but one!
My heart, He would forget.

I questioned him about my love,
that took my very soul;
And with a quiet voice, He said;
It's out of your control

Not everything in life you want, is
given unto Thee;
Your love is true, there is no doubt,
But, it's not meant to be.

I grant you what you need to live,
But, desires I'll not give;
Trust in Me, in time my Son,
A better life you'll live.

I awakened from my dreamy state,
My life had found new peace,
Someday soon, I'll find myself,
My tormented ache will cease.

Shawn Powell

> The love I shared with you was real
> the luster will not pale;
> But now I know I must go on,
> or my heart will surely fail.

AUGUST MOON

THE HEART HAS MANY CHAMBERS

According to Physicians,
our hearts have chambers' four;
Upon an oath they swear on this;
But I believe there's more.

Four chambers pumping breath through veins,
the lifeblood runs its course;
But a Silent Chamber hides quietly,
amongst its surging force.

A dormant chamber small in size,
yet mighty strength it owns;
But the chamber's stirring diligence,
rarely heeds its moans.

Grievous sighs held deep inside,
Awaken with each thought;
The thought of one you loved before,
A love you one time sought.

Though paralyzed the chamber lies,
No movement does it show;
The memoirs of our yesteryear,
is all the chamber knows.

Religiously the chambers churn,
Each Heartbeat strong and true;
They know not why the other sleeps,
they do not have a clue.

For the silent chamber holds on firm,
to the love it knew before;
It cannot revel in it's past, for the
rapture lives no more.

But the Silent Chamber knows its task;
To lie in constant sigh;
For if the chambers knew its pain,
The heart would surely die.

GOODBYE

Goodbye my friend, Goodbye,
Good luck upon your travels;
I'll see you once again, peace be unto you.

Goodbye my love, Goodbye,
Be safe and know, I love you;
I trust you will return, so I may kiss you once again.

Goodbye my precious child,
Goodbye to you for now;
I will always be here,
when you're ready to come home

When my final day is nigh,
and Heaven calls my name,
Do not fear my absence,
for I'll see you once again.

Shawn Powell

STORY POEM III

Shawn Powell

LAVENDER AND ROSES

Wearily, the old man shuffles,
His black shoes aged to gray;
He ascends each step with caution,
with a cane that leads his way.

With eyesight poor, he plots each step
across the marble floor;
Perceptive views are blinding blurs,
No visions to explore.

With each step he listens,
for a whisper in the air;
Faint vibrations chart his course,
the whistles lead him there.

The old man's lonely sojourn,
is amazingly the same;
Lured into the railway house,
to a bench that calls his name.

Shawn Powell

With wrinkled hands, he holds his cane
and rests upon the seat;
His shallow breathing, slowly calmed
by the sound of hasty feet.

People, people, streams of people,
speedily they churn;
But the old man waits for no one,
For there lives no one to yearn.

His soul mate's now an angel,
donned in white with golden bows;
She was taken many years ago,
Yet, his love for her still grows.

The photos of her brilliant face,
have faded with his sight;
He longs to see the flowing gown,
she wore upon their night.

His deafened ears no longer hear,
the melody of their song;
He cannot hear the violins,
that moved them all night long.

AUGUST MOON

He cannot hold her in his arms,
he cannot feel her breath;
He has never loved another,
for his heart she took in death.

The only sense he clings upon
is the essence of her scent;
For this, he makes each labored trek,
to extract one meager hint.

When luck has found its way to him,
a perfumed breeze composes;
A concerto of her fragrances,
soft lavender and roses.

His world is filled with wonder
as he feels her in his soul;
Her celestial voice inflates his
heart, for this instant he is whole.

He sees his bride, her hair in bows,
her body flowing white;
Lavender and Roses, give him
peace to sleep the night.

Shawn Powell

CHAPTER THREE
ROMANCE AND LOVE

Shawn Powell

I underestimated the vastness of my heart
until the day I found true love;
and her soul swam around and through
each chamber of my heart,
and her spirit will continue to swim until
my captured heart beats no more.

WHEN I CLOSE MY EYES

Away I drift in dead of night
as the full moon looms on high

The only sound I faintly hear is
the echo of my heart

When I close my eyes
Dreams embrace my soul

I feel a haunting warmth of blood
transfusing life anew

Enchanted spirits roam within
as your image steals my sight

When I close my eyes
Your essence lights my path

I am drawn into your flame
like a moth is drawn to light

Shawn Powell

Your laughter claims my being
as I bathe inside your smile

I can feel your breath upon my skin
as my pulse begins to quicken

When I close my eyes
I feel the rhythm of your song

Your glory tends the garden
where true beauty can be reaped

And when I close my eyes
I live the dream I long to keep.

ACROSS THE MIDNIGHT SKY

Once upon a time, in a day so
long ago;
A young boy was enchanted by
a girl he longed to know.

Within each ray of early dawn,
His thoughts would often stay;
Hidden behind a face of stone,
His heart was locked away.

Often times he'd daydream,
as two spirits tamed the sky;
Riding on a winged, white steed
Into the night they'd fly.

Billowy puffs of pure white smoke,
would follow every thrust;
They soared amongst the midnight stars,
His wings they learned to trust.

Shawn Powell

The wind whisked through her golden hair,
as she clutched unto his vest;
He could feel her soaring wonder,
as her heart beat through his chest.

The blazing stars grew brighter,
as they sailed above the earth;
And nothing from the world below,
could match their current mirth.

Entangled in a lover's hold,
Their souls became as one;
An inner force, more powerful,
than the eternal burning sun.

Up in to the heavens, and
across the moon above;
They pierced the clouds with laughter
as they raced an ivory dove.

And when they slowed, he'd touch her face,
an angel to behold;
A treasured love, a gift from God,
A story never told.

Startled by reality, Now twenty
years are gone;
And still I wonder of that dream,
the memory surges on.

Guarded in a secret vault,
my dream remains in place;
But sometimes still I feel the chill
of the heavens on my face.

Shawn Powell

ILLUSIONS

The feelings that I have for you
can never be described;
So many songs; but no true words
have ever been transcribed.

Illusions of your elegance,
keep leading me along;
Emotions that control my life,
Thoughts of you so strong.

Affectionate embraces caress
my mind so clear;
Passion floods my sleeping thoughts,
for when I dream, you're here.

When spending time away from you,
my thoughts begin to race;
Visions of you, cloud my head
your sweet, Angelic face.

For when I dream, my treasured
thoughts are brought unto the light;
And descriptions of the love I feel,
are spilled into the night.

My Heart-felt love so precious,
like gemstones in the Earth;
Must also be uncovered to reveal
its splendid worth.

For when love is discovered,
Two lives will start anew;
And build upon the bond they have,
with power known by few.

Until the day our lives are shared,
My life is not complete;
But, hope filled dreams will ease the void
until again we meet.

Shawn Powell

THE REASON FOR THE ROSE

When I gazed upon her,
the first time that we met;
Magnetically my eyes were drawn,
My mind could not forget.

She charmed my very being,
with her elegance and style;
The way she flowed across the room,
Her effervescent smile.

Her dazzling laugh it struck a chord,
A thrill I never had;
Spellbound was my inner soul,
My beguiled mind was mad.

Her sable hair it grazed her back,
as she gently flitted near;
My eyes would not release its hold,
My blood began to sear.

Her gracious way of yielding love,
was featured in her face;
If banned into a lightless void,
her visage I could trace.

I eyed this woman all night long,
but never did we speak;
For this I'm glad, her beauty lives,
No pillaged dream to seek.

Beauty bursts from every flower;
Vivid colors each impose;
And this woman was the reason,
God created every rose.

Shawn Powell

BEAUTY

In the eye of the beholder, Beauty
finds its place;
It touches lives, it fills our souls,
it causes hearts to race.

So many wondrous creations, our
God bestowed this earth;
From Majestic mountains up on high,
to an infant's day of birth.

In my life, I've seen such splendor,
words cannot explain;
How beautiful an Autumn leaf falls
gently to the plain.

Or how the crystal forests, ignite
in morning light;
Causing glistening sparks of ice
to blind your very sight.

AUGUST MOON

Or the crashing waves of salty brine,
upon a blackened rock;
As storm clouds roll along the bay,
splashing rain upon the dock

The Amazing beauty of my grandma,
as she hugs me to her side;
And sweetly pats my rosy cheeks,
Revealing hints of pride.

But the greatest beauty in this
world is shown within a smile;
It captures warmth and drives off fear,
if only for a while.

Celebrating triumph or finding love
sincere;
A Giddy, giggling breath of life is what
I hold so dear.

So laugh unto your heart's content,
No languish shall you find;
For beauty lives within your heart,
your soul and in your mind.

Shawn Powell

Your smile bares your inner charm,
it confesses all your grace;
And nothing is as beautiful,
as the smile upon your face.

My Grandma Dorothy Fite
and my Grandpa Jack Fite

YOUR SMILE

A million smiles clutter minds,
then vanish without thought;
But there is one, with dimpled cheeks
In dreams we all have sought.

Your smiling face it brightens rooms,
with every entrance made;
You warm my heart into a blush,
a hue of rosy shade.

In daytime glow, your smile shines
and makes the sun seem dim;
In Nighttime dark your smile gloats
with confidence so prim.

Reflections of your inner self,
evolve with every smile;
Even through the toughest days,
Your laugh remains in style.

Shawn Powell

And I thank you for your precious
smile, for it means so much to me;
You've given life unto my heart,
which I never thought I'd see.

So trust me with the words I say
that come from deep within;
The warmth your smile's given me,
means friendship 'til the end.

And no matter what evolves in life,
from now until my death;
Engraved upon my heart, I'll know;
Your smile took my breath.

AUGUST MOON

A SINGLE BLADE OF GRASS

My heart does not require hidden
treasures from the sea;
I do not need the riches of the
world to interest me.

My heart does not require precious
jewels to make me smile;
I do not need the riches of the
world to feel worthwhile.

My heart does not require all
the money and its fame;
I do not need the riches of the
world to fan my flame.

A Single Blade of Grass could be
the sweetest gift I know;
As long as it was given by the
one I cherish so.

Shawn Powell

My heart does not require all the
gold this world could give;
But the truth of love upon her lips,
draws each breath, so I might live.

HOW QUICKLY

Lives can change within mere seconds,
Worlds can change, before your eyes;
And, love can find its way to you,
the instance, your heart sighs.

When your heart mislays its pulse,
then quickly feels it tower;
The vacant hole inside your heart
is sealed with wondrous power.

Upon first glance, your spirit's snared,
You question; is it real?
But, then you gaze into her soul,
And her windowed eyes reveal.

That only in your midnight dreams,
has such beauty graced you more;
A flutter, chills your balmy skin,
like a soothing tide on shore.

Her voice breathes life into your blood,
as words tumble from her lips;
You dance inside her laughter,
you thrive within her quips.

You wish the sun would never rise,
so the night could never end;
You never want to see her leave,
for your heart may never mend.

How quickly does the world evolve,
how quickly does it turn;
How quickly does the human heart,
discover one to yearn?

The answers to my tear-stained
prayers, will someday be revealed;
Much like the precious dream I met,
the night my void was sealed.

JUST A SMALL REMINDER

Just a small reminder,
in case you should forget;
You'll always mean the world
to me, I harbor no regret.

I feel your very presence
in all the things I do;
I still can feel a quiver
when my mind envisions you.

I hear your laugh in dead of night,
it jars my very soul;
When it rains, I feel your tears;
Down my face they roll.

I can sense your haunting whispers
as they pierce the summer wind;
I can feel your sultry breathing
as my heart attempts to mend.

Shawn Powell

Inside the mull of the sweltering sun,
I can feel your seething kiss;
My smoldering body reeks of love,
Inside a dark abyss.

I try and try to shut you out,
Attempts are made each day;
But truth be known, I dread the thought,
of your memory washed away.

So, I rise with you each waking dawn,
'til the sun decides to set;
And I give you this reminder, on the
chance, you should forget.

AUGUST MOON

STORY POEM IV

Shawn Powell

AUGUST MOON

MY FRIEND SAM

So many people cross my path,
New friends I meet each day;
Friendly, charming people,
Yet in time they fade away.

My oldest friend from childhood,
Still lives where I was raised;
We grew up playing sports year round,
Our efforts often praised.

A simple friend to say the least,
Eccentric he was not;
Instead of choosing Oreos,
Vanilla wafers hit his spot.

The music that he listened to
were sung in ancient times;
Elvis Presley was his King,
He relished in his rhymes.

Shawn Powell

My Friend Sam, he was not quick,
most jokes he could not get;
He made you laugh so frequently,
by virtue of his wit.

Gracious was his smile,
His eyes, the girls adored;
He was famous for receiving,
the school's "good egg award".

I knew him like a brother,
Inseparable were we;
But, he possessed a certain trait:
Amazing Purity.

Back in High School long ago,
an English class we shared;
We'd read about great artists,
But to Elvis, none compared.

One day the door swung open
and a pregnant teen strolled in;
Rejected by society, this
girl was shamed by sin.

AUGUST MOON

But, my Friend Sam, would take a
stand and offer up his seat;
Cautiously accepting she would
rest her swollen feet.

As days would pass, the baby grew,
and Sam would show his care;
He'd always ask about her health,
his vigilance was rare.

Judged by all whom she would pass,
no smile would she show;
But, My Friend Sam would light her face,
like no other she would know.

His open generosity spread
throughout this learning place;
Encouraged by the hope he gave;
I saw a man of grace.

His heart was worn upon his sleeve,
He knew no other way;
A simple man, who showed his love,
with each smile he'd convey.

Shawn Powell

I wonder if she thinks of him,
though time has passed along;
I wonder if her heart still grooves,
when she hears an Elvis song.

So many people cross my path,
Yet their truth is but a sham;
But, there is one who's heart is pure,
His name is, My Friend Sam.

CHAPTER FOUR
THE AMAZING WORLD OF CHILDREN

Shawn Powell

WHATEVER A WIT MAY BE, I AM AT ITS END,
IT'S AGGRAVATED, IRRITATED, EXASPERATED END;
I CANNOT MOVE A SINGLE LIMB, MY ACHING MIND
IS TAXED;
TANTRUMS SPAWNED FROM HADES, STILL PERMEATE MY
CROWN;
ALAS, THE TODDLER FALLS TO SLEEP,
ALL CUDDLED IN A BALL;
HE HOLDS ON TO HIS TEDDY BEAR, AND SUCKS
UPON HIS THUMB;
I FIND A RENEWED ENERGY AS I KISS HIS
PRECIOUS FACE;
PERFECT LITTLE ANGEL, ALL IS BUT FORGOTTEN.

GOLDEN GRASS OF WINTER

A sweet, little voice answers the phone;
"Hello"
"Hello, my darling Baby Girl."
"Hi Daddy, Where are you?"
"I am now in Delaware, and I'll be here for the week"
"Daddy, where is Delaware, is it far away from me?"

"Delaware, is way up North, where the cold winds meet the ocean"

"Is it near the North Pole, Daddy?"
"No, funny little girl, It is not that far away."

"Will you take me there one day? May I go with you, oh please?"
"Yes, I will take you one day soon, so you can feel the winter on your face."

"Daddy, tell me what's it like?"
"Well, Baby Girl, the air is cold, and the trees have lost their leaves, the wind is whipping through my hair, and the grass is gold, not green."

"The grass is gold up in the north?"

"It is this time of year. But in the spring, the grass turns green and the trees will find their leaves."

"Daddy, I want to go with you and see the golden grass!"

"One day I will bring you here. I miss you very much."

"I miss you too, but I must go, my lunch is getting cold."

"I love you, and I will think of you each minute of the day."

"Bye Daddy, I love you too."

"Bye, Baby Girl."

As the phone line released the call, I sat upon the bed and a single, lonesome tear trickled down my weary face. I miss her bright eyes, her precious smile, her turned up nose and her warm, silly kisses on my cheek. But, no matter where my travels take me; across this mighty world and beyond, my little girl will always be with me, even when the cold, northern winds whip through my hair, as I stand beneath a leafless tree that rests upon the golden grass of winter.

AND WE DANCED...

As a father, I have learned through years,
There is nothing I won't do;
For those whom I protect each day,
My family's love is true.

No matter what the time may show,
or where we all may be;
Requests are made throughout each day,
"The Sacrificial Plea".

One night, my daughter came to me,
Excitement ruled her face;
With vigor she unleashed a task,
Her giddy words would race.

It seemed as though her Brownie Troupe,
was hosting their first dance;
Oh how, her eyes did sparkle,
Disappointment had no chance.

She thanked me time and time again,
as I asked her of the date;
She said it was on Saturday,
at seven, Don't be Late!

That Saturday had soon arrived,
her blonde hair all in curls;
Nervously she inched into the
ballroom filled with girls.

Lil' girls piercing squeals, in
packs they'd run about;
But My Girl held unto my hand,
and never ventured out.

We danced and laughed the whole night
long, our rests were very few;
Ten straight songs would zip right by,
then we'd dance an extra two.

But as the night slowed to an end,
the final dance loomed near;
A saddened face appeared to me,
My thoughts were coming clear.

For as we danced, the final dance,
and I gave her one last twirl;
I realized, that someday soon,
I'd lose My Little Girl.

Eventually a boy her age will
take her from my sight;
And he will dance and laugh with her,
much like we did tonight.

But the one thing he can never take
are the memories of our night;
And I thanked her time and time again,
as the moon beamed down its light.

No matter what the time may show,
or where we all may be;
Always know I'm here for you,
It's my "Sacrificial Plea".

Shawn Powell

THAT FINE DAY

A three-year old with big, brown eyes,
scrambled to her feet;
As she strained to pull her leotards
on her body, so petite.

A pretty pink adorned her frame,
a smile aligned her face;
There was a tiny problem though,
A cause for great disgrace.

For when she put her suit on,
Backwards it would be;
And her tiny lil' biscuits were
exposed for the world to see.

I changed her at the speed of light,
despite her howling way;
Then off to Gymnastics we would go,
upon that one fine day.

AUGUST MOON

I watched from atop the balcony,
that hovered over the gym;
While Autumn stretched with the
other girls, Her giggle full of vim.

The girls lined up, in a zig-zag form,
No straight lines would there be;
With a herd of lil' Pre-school girls,
that's the best you're going to see.

They did their rolls and standard jumps,
they walked the balance beam;
My Autumn would complete each task,
then my name she'd have to scream.

"Hi Daddy," she would shout to me,
as she pranced with cheerful feet;
Then with un-Ladylike precision,
she yanked a wedgie from her seat.

So dainty, yet so unrefined my
precious little girl;
You make your Daddy laugh inside,
as you leap and dance and twirl.

Shawn Powell

I witnessed a daring spirit, as she
flipped into the pit;
I saw a special gift from God;
Her sassy, playful wit.

When the class was finally over,
I received a loving hug;
I held her tight and kissed her cheek,
My heartstrings she would tug.

Out the door, she held my hand,
as we went upon our way;
Then she pulled her final wedgie out,
as I cherished, that fine day.

MY KINDERGARTEN BOY

"Get off the couch, Stay off the bed,
They're not a trampoline;"
"Don't stand so close, Don't get so near,
I'm pumping gasoline."

"Don't pick up snakes or cigar butts,
or chewed up gum that's found;"
"Don't be obscene inside a Church,
For you stand on sacred ground."

"Chew your food, Don't play around
Pork chops aren't a toy;"
It seems I'm always yelling at
My Kindergarten Boy.

"Don't run across the parking lot,
I'd scream until he'd stop;"
"Come out, I'd yell, don't hide from me,"
My heart stops when I shop.

I hope someday he understands the
reasons for my tone;
For if I ever lost my son,
My heart would turn to stone.

Shawn Powell

But, Until that day has come to be,

My voice box will employ;

Those Heartfelt yells of love unto,

My Kindergarten Boy.

LIL' BABY

Lil' Baby tucked inside,
you grow with mommy's love;
Created by two binding souls,
an Angel from above.

You sleep and grow within the womb,
Your mommy's care is true;
We wonder what you'll wear in time,
will it be pink or blue?

Will your hair be donned in ribbons,
Will your clothes be etched in lace?
Will reflections of your mommy's charm,
adorn your precious face?

Or will you grow with speed and
strength, an icon of your sire?
Filling hearts with passion's glow,
'Til laughing faces tire.

Shawn Powell

Will you know the love we feel,
It hangs with each emotion;
Conceived in love, we're in your blood,
we promise true devotion.

And no matter how your life may wend,
Through each, dark and rugged trail;
Live the dreams you long to have,
were with you without fail.

And if you fall down in your path,
No reason should you hide;
Our love you'll find within yourself,
Our love is tucked inside.

AUGUST MOON

HER CANDLE'S FLAME

As life begins, a newborn's shock
is quelled by mother's sighs;
A calming peace engulfs the babe,
soothing frightened cries.

The child knows not where she is,
all objects look the same;
But the mother's gleam is luminous,
much like a candle's flame.

The candle is symbolic, of the
mother's need to bear;
A child of her very own, A love
she longs to share.

The candle's flame appeared the
day, the child was conceived;
Bringing light, unto her sight,
Her soul was now relieved.

Shawn Powell

From the moment of their first embrace,
the candle's flame was pure;
Giving warmth, through cold of night,
A gift so sweet and sure.

As time elapsed, the child walked
along the guiding light;
Down each twisting, turning road,
the candle gave her sight.

Evolving with a changing world,
Her path has gone astray;
Braving lands alone she treks;
But, the candle it must stay.

And someday when the child's grown,
well into her years;
She will look upon the flame,
that tamed her infant tears.

In time, the flame will fade away
and slowly flicker out;
But everlasting love will warm
her heart without a doubt.

AUGUST MOON

And she will know she started
out a dream without a name;
But grew into a dream come true,
much like her candle's flame.

Shawn Powell

LIL' BROWN HAIRED BOY

Lil' Brown Haired Boy;
Your mischief do I yearn;
Your clicking mind so well adept,
How quickly do you learn.

Lil' Blue Eyed Boy;
I long to watch you play;
Your heart so pure, I wonder if,
you think of me each day.

Lil' Brown Haired Boy;
One day you'll be a man;
And then I hope you see my life,
and learn to understand.

That for you I made a sacrifice,
to make your life improved;
The hardest day, I ever had,
the day we were removed.

But, Lil' Blue Eyed Boy;
Worry, will you never;
For the bond I have for you my son,
Never, will I sever.

AUGUST MOON

So live your life with zest and hope,
and don't you dare be sad;
Just know the pride I feel for you;
I love you son, signed Dad.

Shawn Powell

SEVEN HOUR SING-ALONG

Once my lil' girl and I, took
a seven hour drive;
With a three-year old cooped up that long,
could my sanity survive?

I stocked the truck with books and
toys, to keep her entertained;
She also brought some sing-along tapes,
Sheer happiness I feigned.

Her personal mark for sitting still,
was a shade below a minute;
How could she ever make this trip?
my heart was just not in it.

I drove about an hour, as she
played without concern;
Despite her rigid car seat,
that squeezed her with each turn

THEN IT HIT! An Ugly Tone,
complaints of being stuck;
She wanted to jump up and play,
Run amok inside the truck.

I contained her with my right arm,
with my left I steered the wheel:
Her persistence was quite worthy
as she'd kick, and push and squeal

Alas, the memory of the tapes
had finally reached my brain;
I dug inside her backpack,
Any song, I'd not complain!!

Ahhh, the sound of stillness,
her screaming finally ceased;
Thank Goodness for the Kiddie songs:
Our survival rate's increased.

But as I journeyed down the highway,
to this shameful Sing-Song binge;
The ruckus of these dreadful songs
soon made my body cringe.

One more time, she'd bellow out
at the ending of each song;
My head felt like it would implode,
as the truck just sped along.

Finally, with much ado, I searched
inside her pack;
And found a tape that saved my day,
My swiftness would not lack.

I hurriedly removed the tape, and
replaced it with the other;
She was not thrilled about this switch
as she shouted out "Oh Brother."

I said this was a cradlesong, that I sang
when you were born;
Upon my chest you'd fall asleep,
til' the early light of morn.

She looked at me with big, brown
eyes and smiled bashfully;
Her cheeks were flush, she gnawed her lip,
her eyes stared tenderly.

AUGUST MOON

The soothing sound of yesterday,
when she'd suckle on her thumb;
I pictured my sweet angel, bound
in blankets, as I'd hum.

The lyrics drifted sweetly, up to heaven,
Notes were soaring;
That's when my precious darling said:
"Hey Dad, This song is BOR-ING!"

Well I love you too, Honey!!

Shawn Powell

A FATHER'S LOVE

Miraculous: the word that's used
to describe an infant's birth;
Cannot be matched by anything,
created on this Earth.

A precious cry that whimpers out,
is music to the ears;
The little fingers and tiny toes,
will melt your eyes with tears.

The little toddler grows with speed,
as changes become clear;
The snowflake hair is spun to gold,
you see yourself appear

But then one day through no one's fault,
Lives begin to break;
Damaged hearts, broken dreams
are lost inside a quake.

You wonder how you'll ever cope
and face another day;
Without the angel of your world
who brings each morning ray.

A hollow beating in your heart
will chill your body cold;
The clay of life you brought to be,
never will you mold.

But love, sweet love will conquer all,
and chase away the sorrow;
You'll build upon both hope and faith,
and pray for each tomorrow.

To see my baby smile,
or to hear her tender voice;
Gives me peace so I might live,
beyond this painful choice.

As I lay upon my back at night,
my heavy eyelids close;
God is looking over us,
Her Father: I was chose.

A Father's love is infinite,
it soars beyond the stars;
And veiled behind her charming grace,
Her smile hides our scars.

Shawn Powell

GO TO SLEEP MY CHILDREN

Go to sleep my baby,
close your weary eyes;
You are safe, for I am here,
to quell your lonely cries.

Through the soft pink blanket,
I can see your heaving chest;
I'll check on you throughout the night,
so let your body rest.

Go to sleep my little boy,
Close your eyes, I pray;
You are safe, for I am here,
Your nightmare's gone away.

Dream of making snowmen,
Dream of kickball games outside;
Dream a dream of you and I,
as we journey side by side

Go to sleep my teenage girl,
close your eyes and sleep;
You are safe for I am here,
Your beauty runs so deep.

Dream until the morning sun
decides to meet the day;
Dream about your future,
while refreshing yesterday.

Go to sleep my children,
close your weary eyes;
You are safe, for I am here,
To quell your lonely cries.

And I will dream a dream of you,
that will last throughout the night;
And then I'll meet you once again,
when dawn retrieves its light.

Shawn Powell

STORY POEM V

Shawn Powell

JIM

I remember climbing up the stairs
into his fourth floor room;
His office, dank and eerie,
it reeked of death and gloom.

For months I'd heard the stories,
A freak they all would muse;
A laughingstock he was to them,
He lingered in abuse.

A mammoth of a human being,
His weight five-twenty two;
He stood about six-seven,
and his life was nearly through.

I took a seat beside him, as he
spilled into his chair;
His ashy face and sweat-soaked
skin, would match his oily hair.

Shawn Powell

He knew his days were numbered,
His health a dying flame;
He needed life infused in him,
for the Reaper knew his name.

I heard the laughter in my head,
as I sat alongside Jim;
The haunting chortles he endured,
upon each mocking whim.

His pain was shown between each
breath, as he slowly spoke his mind;
He'd have to stop from time to time,
to let his thoughts unwind.

He choked with tears upon request,
of a service I could give;
He wanted me to help him have,
one normal year to live.

I stared into the eyes of Jim,
and told him I was here;
I'd help him out no matter what,
My eyes released his fear.

AUGUST MOON

Jim commenced his journey,
Showing courage with each stride;
Carefully, I pushed this man,
and I never left his side.

Within two years, Jim had lost,
One hundred-sixty pounds;
His smile burned more calories,
than all his walking rounds.

But still the ignorance of our world
would rear its ugly head;
And those who did not know this
man, would snicker while he tread.

Then the day had come to be,
I left Jim to his own;
My life moved on, but Jim remained,
He'd walk his path alone.

I never saw him from that point on,
although I would check in;
Gradually his work slowed down,
His weight he'd gain again.

Shawn Powell

A year had passed and so did Jim,
His heart could take no more;
His loss was sad, but I rejoiced,
I watched his spirit soar.

I know Jim left contented, for in
two years, his soul did mend;
But more than that, he left relieved,
Their laughter now would end.

CHAPTER FIVE
THOUGHTS ON LIFE

Shawn Powell

How many tattered shoes must we discard,
before the silver-robed magistrates of our
lives, lay down their noisome gavels?

THE LITTLE THINGS

As a newborn cherub, cuddled tight
in your mother's snug embrace;
Precious, tiny kisses find their
way upon your face.

Little whirs and plaintive sighs,
so faint, but yet so strong;
We'd melt our parent's loving hearts,
as they rocked us all night long.

As a toddler in this mighty world,
the small things held such awe;
The slinky toy, the bounding frog,
A puppy's playful paw.

A little chin all covered up, in a beard
of Eskimo Pie:
Chasing bubbles in the yard;
The blinking firefly.

Shawn Powell

Completing crooked somersaults to
an audience of two;
The joyous sounds of their applause,
would warm us through and through.

Throughout our days, we roam about
in a world that's grown too great;
The little things in life are gone,
Our memories lie in wait.

From the innocent views of an infant,
to the id of a complex teen;
To a person in their thirties,
or an age that comes between.

Through the cycle of a thing called life,
we all will soon return;
To the little things in life we've missed,
And we will then discern.

The enchantment of a smile,
or a baby's loving coo;
Binds our very spirit to the soul
that we once knew.

AUGUST MOON

For we have grown into this world,

and a mighty world it be;

Yet nothing holds more wonder

than the little things to me.

My mother Rita Kallal holding her son

Shawn Powell

HINT OF LIGHT

Have you ever pondered, where our
memories make their home;
Brilliant swirls in dull gray matter,
steadily they roam.

Reserved inside each chasm, with all
memories locked away;
Awaiting tiny hints of light to bring
them out one day.

Objects or perhaps events, remind
us of the past;
Names and faces, good and bad,
forever they will last.

Safe and sound, the memories live,
awaiting their return;
To be recalled, in idle chat,
A hint of light they yearn.

HAVE YOU EVER??

Have you ever had to say farewell,
to the idol of your world;
Knowing he will never see your
total life unfurled?

Have you ever had to leave someone
who takes with her, your heart?
A silent clamor dwells within,
as sacred dreams depart.

Have you ever had to watch in tears,
as your child leaves your life?
Her final hug is all that saves your
drowning soul from strife.

You kiss her face, and choke on fear,
as they pry her fingers free;
You cannot feel, for you are numb,
Your teary eyes can't see.

Shawn Powell

Have you ever laid upon your bed,
as your body shook with pain;
The pain of loss, the pain of guilt.
Your drifting mind insane.

Why must we all endure such pain,
Why must we all endure?
Love is stronger than a mountain.
More than snow, all love is pure.

Like a stream my love flows on and on,
'til it meets the waterfall;
My life is greater, to have loved then lost,
than to have never loved at all.

THE SPIRIT OF THE GAME

The price one pays to hone a skill,
and learn a trait so well;
Unknowingly prepares a life,
for future times to tell.

Moving snow off a concrete slab,
in weather cold as ice;
Just to shoot the ball in gloves,
through air my breath would slice.

In heat that poured upon my skin,
while soles burned on the 'phalt;
Giving all, while sun scorched skies,
turned body sweat to salt.

And no matter where the game was played,
perfection was the dream;
To stick the J, or dish the rock,
to play to one's extreme.

Shawn Powell

At times, when shots were raining in
from everywhere I'd aim;
Though target swift, still I missed
the Spirit of the Game.

In all the hoops I scored for years,
I failed to see the signs;
For the meaning of this game I played,
Lay not between the lines.

It hangs not in the cheer of fans,
who applaud from play to play;
It's not in loss or victory,
no matter what they say.

But in the color of the game, is
where the spirit lives;
Every man; no matter race, his
heart he always gives.

No difference is there made in tones;
We blend into a team;
For when the uni's worn with pride,
We see just red or green.

AUGUST MOON

For it is the perfect union;

All colors are the same;

And I thank the Lord for showing me,

The Spirit of the Game.

Spirit of the Game at Southwestern High School in Piasa, Illinois

Shawn Powell

THIS MOUNTAIN THAT YOU SEE

Down the trail you wander, your mind
a cluttered mess;
Your thoughts explore confusion, that
your lips dare not confess.

Your afflicted heart gets heavier,
with each gasp of air you breathe;
Each night time star impales your soul,
Inside this flame you seethe.

Your troubled eyes reveal your pain,
you fear the great unknown;
But trust in love and friendship,
for inside your heart it's sewn.

The wish of those who love you,
is to numb you from your sorrow;
Just enough so you may find,
your reason for tomorrow.

AUGUST MOON

For now you must go onward, for
your path call's unto thee;
You'll need your strength, so you may climb,
This mountain that you see.

And when you've reached the apex,
and the rocky path's no more;
Your life will be much grander,
than the life you knew before.

Shawn Powell

RELIEF

Wilted greens succumbing
to the weight of a newborn frost;
Appreciated comfort;
The ragweed pollen lost.

I now can breathe in glorious air,
that no longer pricks my nose;
No more wretched sneezing
when the dandelion blows.

Icy air, I welcome you,
take all the time you need;
Then I'll wish you on your way, when
the spring wind spreads its seed.

ELEGANT FLAME

Elegant flame rising and falling
from the wick you breathe in life
The scented heat melts like lava
as shards of wax slink down your side
Effulgent light causing shadows
casting movements in the night
Breathe the air so you might live
and burn through pitch-black clouds
Elliptical blaze, swirl and dance
so you may dominate your fear
of the ever-looming blackened skies
that will someday snuff your star

Shawn Powell

THE KEY TO HAPPINESS

Happiness, the key to life
without it, who are we?
An answer to life's riddle,
Is an individual plea.

A smile is our lighthouse,
It's our beacon in the night;
It lifts the murk that covers us,
revealing precious light.

Laughter that exists within,
must burst without refrain;
We must allow this to occur,
Like clouds permit the rain.

For dampened spirits whittle lives,
into small flecks of pain;
Depressing rivers flow amid
the lifeblood we sustain.

AUGUST MOON

Until a joyous smile can
enlighten hearts of stone;
True happiness will hide away
inside its weary moan.

The riddle can't be answered
when your world's bereft of light;
Nebulous skies shall burn away,
When your lighthouse quells the night.

Shawn Powell

STORY POEM VI

Shawn Powell

FROZEN TEARS

I dream a dream that bores my heart,
no matter what the year;
I still can see the images, so vivid
and so clear.

It happened on a wintry day when I
was just a teen;
The falling snowflakes tumbled down,
as white pre-empted green.

Excused from classes on this day,
the streets were paved in ice;
A blizzard was the forecast:
Children scurried much like mice.

Upon the bus we were corralled
to the heated scent of youth;
Raucous grunts and foolish games,
our minds were so uncouth.

Shawn Powell

I stared outside my window as the
mass soon disappeared;
But standing in the blinding snow
one lonely soul appeared.

A frail and crippled little girl,
each leg in heavy brace;
She staggered on the icy walk,
As terror ruled her face.

I could not move out of my seat,
despite the stabbing pain,
That marred my inner being,
As I watched her body strain.

She fell upon the hardened ice,
but, could not rise from there;
Her eyes burned holes right through my soul,
as she struggled in despair.

Finally, my nerve arrived, and I
jumped out of my seat;
But then the bus was thrown in gear,
and I stalled on silent feet.

AUGUST MOON

I looked outside the window as
the bus roared down it's path;
My heart was numb, I failed this girl,
I fumed inside self-wrath.

I saw a broken spirit of a human
just like me;
I did not lend a hand to her, How could
I let this be?

A teacher found this helpless child,
forsaken by her peers;
A frigid heap of flesh and steel,
was drenched in frozen tears.

My saddest day without a doubt;
The girl upon the ice;
Her sobbing eyes of horror,
still reflect as visions splice.

I am human, this is true,
A mortal I will err;
But, never should a blizzard
blind the eyes, of those who care.

Shawn Powell

CHAPTER SIX
REFLECTIONS OF MYSELF

Shawn Powell

Reflections of those who have touched my world,
Can be found in the mirrors of my soul.
They are sewn into the fibers of my very being,
And will forever live in the pages of my life.

MY HERO

A question once was posed to me,
when I was just a youth;
A question that required thought;
Earnest seeking truth.

Who Is Your Hero? was the query
subjected unto me;
At first, I thought the answer would
be easy as could be.

But then the names of whom I thought,
equated hero lore;
Soon multiplied to many names,
Celebrities galore.

I thought of Davy Crockett, the King
of the Wild Frontier;
I thought of valiant men of war,
I thought of Paul Revere.

I thought of Gentle Abe, and the
hatred he'd oppose;
I thought of Samson's mighty strength,
he battled awesome foes.

I thought of Jackie Robinson, and
what he did for Sports;
I thought of Pistol Pete's techniques,
The Wizard of the Courts.

I recognized the quandary, that this
question put me in;
So, I took my problem to my Dad,
for his input on these men.

My Dad, he studied every name,
I had written on my sheet;
And he agreed, this Hero list,
was awfully hard to beat!

He laid the list upon the desk,
and grabbed the Dictionary;
He looked up Hero in its text,
His actions would not tarry.

The word revealed a Hero as a
person who is brave;
Sacrificing his own life, for
others he might save.

The word revealed a leader,
courageous with each act;
A Hero would protect his own,
Pure loyalty intact.

And as my father finished,
My answer came to be;
For the Hero, I was looking for,
stood in front of me.

For the basis of a Hero,
Is quite difficult to seek;
To protect and love and sacrifice,
A Hero is unique!

And as I proudly answered, the
question posed to me;
I looked into my Father's eyes,
It was easy as could be.

For my father, Bobby Powell

Shawn Powell

My Hero, my father Bobby Powell

AUGUST MOON

GREEN BEAN COOKIES

Oh, every holiday was grand,
when it came to Grandma's sweets;
She could pull your spirits up each time,
with a single tray of treats.

Chocolate pie with cool whip topping,
Peach pie al a mode;
Apple thins were iced so smooth,
in her Wonka-like abode.

Lemon, Lime and Coconut Pie,
they donned a sweet meringue;
My mouth would start to salivate,
with each dinner bell that rang.

Puddings, Custards and ice cream cones
would melt right down your throat;
Texas cake with fresh walnuts,
were chased by a root beer float.

Then one day the pies just stopped,
Much to my chagrin;
For Grandma had retired her most
famous rolling pin.

Grandma tried to make it up, by baking
other things;
Among the many morsels tried were
Pizza Rolls and Wings

Then my Grandma had a plan,
And Cookies were the solution;
But we're not talking cookie, We're
talking, cookie revolution.

She dumped into her batter,
every chip that she could find;
Chocolate, Peanut Butter,
Any chip, She didn't mind.

One day, I took a bite of one, with
Pineapple chunks and a cherry;
Cashew nuts and butterscotch
chips and hint of Frankenberry.

AUGUST MOON

I jokingly asked my Grandma
if she could add some fresh green beans;
From out of the pantry she emerged, with
Green Giant providing the means

But only after many years did I figure
out the reason;
Why the cookies took the place of pie,
for every holiday season.

Her arthritic hands could not take, the
shaping of the pies;
So she bought the pre-made cookies,
and created each surprise.

She showed her love with every chip,
and every berry picked each fall;
And the Green Bean Cookie, has since
remained, her sweetest treat of all.

for my Grandmother, Dorothy Fite

Shawn Powell

THE HOUSE ON PIERCE

On the eastern side of a street called
Pierce, a decrepit cottage stood;
In a college town all broken homes,
were in this neighborhood.

Inside a house of white-wash paint,
Six fellows dwelled within;
No welcome mat was visible; A sign
said "Come on In".

The crooked steps, with broken planks
led towards the door;
The screen door flapped in gusty breeze
the doorbell worked no more

Long, brown sheets of plywood wrapped
throughout the inside walls;
Floors were warped, carpet stained,
the wind whipped through the halls.

AUGUST MOON

The kitchen smelled of grease and grime,
the ceilings scarred with smoke;
The window panes were lined with cracks
leaving ledges soaked.

The bedrooms of this shameless place
were cramped in A-Frame slope;
The box springs set on concrete blocks,
Their backs would learn to cope.

Harsh winters chilled them to the bone,
In coats, they'd sleep at night;
Mice would roam throughout their home,
amidst the night time light.

This House imperfect, though it seemed,
a marred and anguished shell;
For men, a hull that captured hope,
For others it was hell.

For the lives of those who dwelled inside,
this House of damaged rooms;
Did not fall or end their lives,
these rooms were not their tombs.

Their lofty goals were evident;
they contemplated fate;
They knew the work ahead of them;
Their perfect life must wait.

For the house portrayed the men within;
An empty shell in need;
To fill a void and rise above,
an environment they'd heed.

Accomplishing a goal as this,
to escape impoverished fear;
Their perseverance must evolve,
for then their future's clear.

They understood the consequence
to choose the easy road;
Though rough and rocky was their path,
They learned from their abode.

For wisdom was their claim from school,
their minds completely fit;
But through the lessons of this house,
Their tunnel's light was lit.

AUGUST MOON

All lives are resurrected, if
hope's allowed to dwell;
From degradation, they arrived,
They filled their empty shell.

for Kerry, Bill, Deron, Dan and Mike

Shawn Powell

A BROTHER'S LOVE

Brethren on this Earth,
we all can claim as men;
But when the bond is shared in
blood, it is hard to comprehend.

A complex love that Brothers share,
Affections rarely shown;
But tied into the soul of man,
the love is always known.

A Brother's love sewn deep inside,
with instincts of protection;
A love of sacrificial debt,
that yearns for true perfection.

For the strength that's built through
Brotherhood, is mired through the core;
And a Brother's love will never die,
the love's worth dying for.

For Chuck and Corey

AUGUST MOON

ODE TO THE BOSS

A General of all companies,
true to victory;
Born to be a leader he wields
his mighty sword,
A master of his destiny;
Demander of his fate;
Provider to his family,
Sentry to his gate.
In constant search for loyalty
he looks for men of valor;
Stand with him in triumph,
or fall unto his blade;
For he will lead the onslaught,
And rise above the rest;
And from this bloodied battleground,
you'll fall upon one knee,
All hail, unto the Boss!
All hail, All hail, to thee!

A tribute to George Steinbrenner

Shawn Powell

MAN OF STEEL

From conception, 'til the birth of one
who's life was never planned;
He showed his love without regard,
he lent this boy his hand.

Small fingers wrapped 'round calloused
hands, a grip so soft yet firm;
It captured warmth that spread
for years, a love he would confirm.

As years went by I watched a man,
who showed me how to fight;
Fight for family, Fight for love,
Fight for what is right.

His labor of love, showed in his sweat
he slaved in searing heat;
The Earth would thicken on his neck,
as he walked his fields of wheat.

On tractor green, he powered through
long rows of Harvest Gold;
His heart so strong, he never failed
no matter rain or cold.

AUGUST MOON

He pushed himself to be the source;
To be the very best;
He strived through sickness and through
pain, and with little rest.

At dusk, he'd end another day,
with his body beaten down;
But, still he'd come into the house
and be my smiling clown.

I idolized this Man of Steel,
he gave my life such joy;
He showed me everyday he lived,
I'd always be his boy.

And on the day this man decides
to leave this World behind;
I hope he looks into my eyes,
and knows I'm of his kind.

I will fight for love and honor,
His truth I understand;
For what he did, I'll not forget;
He lent this man his hand.

For Jack Fite

Shawn Powell

The Mighty Ship, My Grandpa Jack Fite

TRUE FRIEND

The secret of a Friendship,
so many fail to find;
The search goes on from year to year,
but visually we're blind.

To see the truest quality
that invokes our total trust,
A True Friend always lends an ear,
for virtue is a must.

A True Friend helps one laugh away,
the tears that well within;
A True Friend calmly disagrees,
if sin he feels your in.

For friends will come into your path
from every walk of life;
Some will bring great joy to you,
while others cause you strife.

Shawn Powell

And though these friends seem dear
at heart, sadly none will be;
But, the friend of truth will
brave the fire and soothe your agony.

Within a misty web of haze,
A True Friend's light will shine;
And lead you to a life of truth,
A truth that's quite divine.

For a Friendship shared by two
true souls, will never seek an end.
The friendship will forever thrive,
As a truly matchless blend.

AUGUST MOON

STORY POEM VII

Shawn Powell

PAINTED SMILES

Tiny beads of moisture popped from
above my blondish brows;
My wrinkled forehead tensing from
internal, childish vows.

Diligent fingers painted features of
a cocker spaniel pup;
Varnish flying on a wooden base,
as the brush stroked down then up.

After the initial coat of varnish
dried with streaking flaws;
Four hanging hooks were then installed,
below the puppy's paws.

The final step of this arduous task,
Ne'er could I reverse;
On to the doggie's chest, I'd seal,
A treasured Bible verse.

Shawn Powell

This imperfect token that I made,
back when I was seven;
Was created during Bible School,
as I learned of God in Heaven.

The little varnished puppy, would
suspend each unused belt;
Displaying all the choices, for
the waist of one so svelte.

I beamed much like the smile
that I painted on its face;
For I knew the lil' Puppy,
would enjoy my Grandpa's place.

I left the church that very day,
with my creation wrapped in white;
I could not wait to share this gift,
with my Grandpa on that night.

As my mother pulled up to his farm,
I bolted from my seat;
I jumped the hedge, without remorse,
as I'd land on running feet.

But, I failed to find him in the house
so I sprinted to the shed;
Down the steps and through the yard,
to a clanging sound ahead.

I watched him wield his hammer
as I hid behind the door;
With nervous hands, I giggled for
this present he'd adore.

But then the hammer missed its mark
and struck my Grandpa's thumb
He whirled and yelled profanities,
a demon, he'd become.

Quietly I backtracked, then I spun
and ran away;
I threw the Puppy in the trash,
as my Mother turned to say;

"Was that your Dog, you threw away?"
Reluctantly, I'd nod;
I told her that he'd hate it, 'cause I heard
him curse out God.

Shawn Powell

My Mother smirked and then explained,
that people make mistakes;
She said that Grandpa loves the Lord,
No matter what he breaks.

Then my Grandpa made his way
into the stairway hall;
With teary eyes, I glared at him
as he hung it on the wall.

He told me he'd been searching for a
Hound to hold his belt;
Then he smiled and winked at me,
though his thumb was one big welt.

Soon my tears had vanished as he
held me to his side;
He said that he was sorry for the words
that he let slide.

People are imperfect, we will make
mistakes and err;
But, do not judge another,
for we all have sins we bear.

AUGUST MOON

The year my Grandpa passed away,
I walked his stairway hall;
And there the little varnished dog
still lived upon the wall.

For twenty-seven years, he used this
puppy every day;
The verse had yellowed through the years,
but the meaning, it would stay.

Just like the lacquered puppy,
He too has found his place;
I know this, for his spirit paints
the smiles on my face.

Shawn Powell

CHAPTER SEVEN
MUSICAL LYRICS

Shawn Powell

NO PLACE TO GO

There was a man, his name was Emery,
He had a wife and a son named Joe;
They lived in peace, but starved through famines,
They had no life, No place to go.

Until one day, He'd load his wagon,
with precious cargo, his wife and son;
They ventured westward, to the uncombed valleys,
so they could settle, where the antelopes run.

They came upon a mighty river,
No place to cross, No place to go;
He entered into the raging current,
but lost his grip in the undertow.

He watched them drift down the mighty river,
He tried to save them, as the winds would blow;
He battled bravely in the muddy waters,
He watched them plunge to their graves below.

AUGUST MOON

His heart was black, his soul was empty,

his mind was numb, with all the pain;

For Emery saved, himself from drowning,

but his poor heart, he'd never regain.

He watched them drift down the mighty river,

He tried to save them, as the winds would blow;

He battled bravely in the muddy waters,

He watched them plunge to their graves below.

He failed to save them, so he now surrenders,

to the mighty river, No place to go.

Shawn Powell

IF I HAD YOU

In a small cafe, nestled on the beach
of a Golden Shore;
A young man made of millions, often
entered through the door.

He would visit every month or so,
On business he'd fly in;
He would always stop in for bite,
and then he'd leave again.

Alone this bachelor traveled,
yet never would he date;
But, on this day of destiny, the
man would meet his fate.

For the girl who served his dinner,
made his mind completely race;
His eyes were filled with wonder,
as he stared upon her face.

AUGUST MOON

and he said…
If I had you, all your problems,
would simply fade away;
If I had you, I'd take care of you
each and every day;

For my life would be much richer,
If I could hold you next to me;
If I had you, I would love you,
throughout eternity.

Many months had passed along, and
the man still flew to her;
He knew she was the one for him
inside his heart would stir.

For his Father always told him,
To trust with all his might;
For the girl that he would one day love,
He'd find upon first sight.

But still the girl she pushed away,
Her feelings she'd not show;
Her heart was saying yes to him,
Her head was saying no.

Shawn Powell

For the life that he would offer,
was one she could not live;
He had all and she had nothing,
what could she ever give?

but, he said…
If I had you, all your problems
would simply fade away;
If I had you, I'd take care of you,
each and every day;

For my life would be much richer,
If I could hold you next to me;
If I had you, I would love you,
throughout eternity

One night, the man got up to leave,
and he touched her on the hand;
One day soon, he said to her,
She too would understand.

But later, in a misty sky, his plane
would not take flight;
And he crashed upon the treetops,
that dark and grisly night.

AUGUST MOON

Awakened by a phone call
she rushed unto his side;
With her first sight of him helpless,
Her eyes were opened wide.

In a coma he lay paralyzed
as she sat upon his bed;
And she held his hand up to her
heart and this is what she said;

If I had you all your problems
would simply fade away;
If I had you, I'd take care of you,
each and every day

For my life would be much richer
if I could hold you next to me;
If I had you, I would love you
throughout eternity

…And as she finished speaking,
he squeezed her hand so tight;
And she would finally understand,
she loved him at first sight.

Shawn Powell

AUGUST MOON

STORY POEM VIII

Shawn Powell

NINE LIVES

It's been said from days of old,
that cats possess nine lives;
Escaping perilous fates of doom
the feline proudly thrives.

I know this theory must speak truth,
for my family's cat was one;
Who liberated himself from death,
His days were never done.

But one day in the early spring,
as a farmer plowed his field;
Tomcat Tom just disappeared,
No clues would this cat yield.

My family combed the countryside,
and called his name out loud;
But the ray of hope was growing dim,
behind a blotting cloud.

Shawn Powell

After many grueling days, exploring
foolish leads;
We halted the search for Tomcat Tom,
despite my siblings pleads.

Many days had passed on by, when a
friend and I played catch;
Hurling wild fastballs, the game of catch
turned into fetch.

Between my legs the ball would whiz,
and rest in furrowed dirt;
A fresh, plowed field of rich, black silt
adorned my new white shirt.

But, when I once retrieved the ball,
I heard a muted sound;
I did not know its origin, but it
came from underground.

I yelled unto my ole' friend Ron,
"There's something in this field;"
He said that I was crazy, in a
chair, I should be wheeled.

AUGUST MOON

Quickly I uncovered all the blades
of giant soil;
To the faded mews of Tomcat Tom,
his body in a coil.

Tom denied his own demise, his
life was spared again;
How many lives has this cat lived?;
I swore, it must be ten.

Ecstatic girls came running, as he
crawled out from below;
His body resembled an accordion,
as he zithered to and fro.

As I watched his feeble body try to
walk in glaring sun;
I wondered why, cat's lives were
nine, but people only one.

Buried by our worldly woes,
God rescues us from strife;
Eternal bliss on Streets of Gold,
our reward for just one life.

Shawn Powell

CHAPTER EIGHT
HUMOROUS TALES

Shawn Powell

IF YOU HAVE NEVER SHED A TEAR, THEN YOU
WILL NEVER KNOW HOW IT TRULY
FEELS TO LAUGH.

SUMMER'S GLOW

On the warmest day of June,
in the year of Double Seven;
We stood upon a field of clay,
A Little Leaguer's Heaven.

Perched upon the left field fence,
the orange sun did fall;
And soon the lights would send down
beams, a gleaming path for all.

People flowed into the park,
To heed their children's glory;
Champions declared this night:
The Local Headline story.

We scanned the crowd and popped our
mitts, we chewed our gum with fury;
Butterflies on a Caffeine High,
made us wish they'd hurry.

Shawn Powell

The time was nigh, we grabbed our gloves
and stared into the night;
With hats pulled down above our brows
we clenched our teeth real tight.

As we took the field that evening,
The horizon lost it's glow;
Behind the bullpen out in left,
Where, we did not know?

Our coaches feared the worst it seemed,
and players mocked their view;
With four of our best players gone,
What was our team to do?

We started eight instead of nine,
Outfielders…only two;
We prayed to God Almighty;
Any help would do.

Our Infield was our Outfield,
our Outfield was our subs;
One wore glasses, but could not see,
the other's name was Tubs.

AUGUST MOON

The diamond's grass was neatly trimmed,
the mound was like a mountain;
I saw ole' Tubs chug a snow cone down,
behind the dugout fountain.

We took the field in Orange shirts,
with trim of White and Black;
The team we played was decked in Blue,
Gold letters lined their backs.

I stood upon the rubber high,
and glared down to my foe;
My windup quick, I reared straight
back and offered up one low.

Two runs were scored in inning one,
on errors count them three;
A ball to Jimmy out in right,
had caromed off his knee.

Tubs in left, misplayed a roller
that glanced off of his cleats;
Interrupting thoughts of food,
Concession dreams of treats.

We battled back from that point on,
but failed to score a run;
We trailed into our last at bat,
Two runs against our none.

The final inning; Pressure's On;
The pitcher's throwing fire.
The first two batters that he'd face,
he'd easily retire.

The Game looked grim all smiles gone,
Next batters six through eight;
Our family members folded chairs,
Some headed for the gate.

The coach at third he looked upon
the batters due to hit;
And pulled them to the outside fence,
he would not let them quit.

He looked at Jimmy batting sixth,
and Tubs who followed after;
And said with sternness to them both,
"Ignore their nagging laughter."

"Just grit your teeth and swing your
bats like lightning hits the sky;
And run like deer until you score,
we're with you do or die."

Jimmy strolled up to the dish,
and took a widened stance;
The pitcher grinned from ear to ear,
This was his perfect chance.

To end the game without a flaw,
He'd shut the Bengals down;
But on a pitch he threw outside,
His grin became a frown.

Jimmy singled down the right field line,
as the ball skimmed off the bag;
He clapped his hands with fervency,
His spirit would not lag.

With beads of moisture on his face,
Tubs knew that he was next;
His hits were few all season long,
He swore his bat was hexed.

He gripped his bat into his hands,
as a Demonic mug appeared;
Engulfed into the Black of Night,
the ball soon disappeared.

With sloth-like speed he galloped
onward, fearing for his fate;
He rounded second; He could not stop;
The relay headed straight.

But, luck would have it on this night,
Tubs' triple caused a wreck;
He crashed into the third base bag,
the ball glanced off his neck.

When the dust had cleared at third,
One run was finally scored.
The corner man gimped 'round the bag,
Tubs confidence had soared.

The coach grabbed Billy from On-Deck,
His reliance was quite meek;
He hadn't got a hit all year,
Aggressiveness was weak.

AUGUST MOON

He told young Billy, "I know your fear,
I've been here once before.
But take a breath; Close your eyes,
and lean o'er the plate some more."

Inside the box, he stood so still,
a statue he portrayed;
A boy who never reached First Base,
in all the years he played.

Two strikes zipped by, without a blink,
No movement did he show;
But on the next pitch, Billy leaned,
and took one off his 'bow.

His eyes welled up with drops of tears,
his elbow swelled up tight;
But the cheer for his heroic stance,
would ring throughout the night.

As Billy waltzed his way to first
the pain began to cease;
His pride rang true; His job was done;
His heart had found its peace.

Shawn Powell

With runners on the corner, Two outs
still loomed about;
The pitcher mopped his sweaty brow,
He needed just one out.

The leadoff batter, 0 for three,
His average was much better;
He saw the fastball darting in and
he read it like a letter.

He lined the ball deep in the gap,
Speed was on his side;
Valiantly, Tubs spanned the plate,
the score had just been tied.

Billy sped around the base path,
Unfamiliar was this route;
The leadoff batter closing fast,
He bellowed out a shout.

Billy's face, strained with pain,
as he rounded past third base;
The ball approached from Outfield
skies, but Billy dove with grace.

AUGUST MOON

As Billy glared up to the ump,
His mouth was spilling dirt;
Two arms came out and shouted safe,
He cried, but was not hurt.

Dramatically, the game was won,
No feeling could compare;
Through stress and pain we battled on,
To quit, we would not dare.

I saw a difference in the boys who
played that crucial hour;
Nerves of Steel convinced them all,
their gift of inner power.

A reborn faith had captured them;
True Victory was abound;
For boys grew into men that night,
The horizon's glow was found.

For the Brighton Bengals of 1977

Shawn Powell

The Bengals of Brighton, Illinois, 1977

MY GRANDMA THE PITCHER

"Come on Son, dinner's on, let's
eat before it's cold."
I raced out from the living room,
doing as I was told.

I took a seat at the kitchen table,
As Grandma filled my plate;
Fried taters, ham and s'gettios
and boy did it smell great!

My father would be coming soon,
to take me to my game;
I ate, as Grandma raced around;
The stove was one big flame.

Eat up boy, you need your strength,
to play your game tonight;
I covered my food with ketchup and salt,
and washed it down with Sprite.

Then my Grandma bugged my eyes,
with a startling tale of lore;
She claimed she pitched for the Woodburn
Boys in the year of thirty-four.

Shawn Powell

She said she threw a drop ball, then she
showed her famous grip;
A sinking, sliding splitter, that caused
her foes to trip.

But then she went a bit too far, with her
Amazing Baseball fable;
For this fireball at four foot ten, made
me fall right from the table.

With my Grandpa in the other room
His hearing not the best;
He Jumped from his Recliner, she had
ended his short rest.

She said she struck poor Grandpa out
three times in just one game;
Steam poured from my Grandpa's ears,
as he tried to stake his claim.

You never struck me out three times
what planet are you from?
I stared at my sweet Grandma,
A liar she'd become.

I couldn't bear the agony, my Grandma's
fibs weren't nice;
But then my Grandpa belted out,
"You struck me out, Just twice!"

My head spun 'round in amazement,
Her story had rung true;
"Wow, poor Grandpa must of stunk
to be struck out by you."

My Grandma then instructed me to
grab my glove and ball;
And told me to go run outside,
as she raced down through the hall

As I waited for her by the elm, she
darted through the trees;
In a skirt, with bright white shoes,
and nylons to her knees

She grabbed the ball and showed her
grip, as she lobbed it to me slow;
Gravity would pull it down, as I
caught the ball down low

Shawn Powell

"See how it drops, right to the ground
I haven't lost my skills!"
Grandpa yelled from on the porch,
"I'll fetch your arthritis pills!"

"OH phooey", she smirked, then looked
my way, and said "Go grab that bat."
I said "No way, I will not swing,
You can't make me do that"

She told me not to worry, no contact
would I make;
Reluctantly I grabbed the club;
This was a huge mistake.

My thoughts were spinning crazily,
As I walk up to the box
One hard hit and I'd knock poor
Granny, right out of her nylon socks.

What to Do? What to Do?
A jumbled mess indeed;
Maybe I could feign a death,
or get my nose to bleed.

When suddenly it came to me,
A stellar plan, I'd yield
I'd swing real hard and pull the ball,
Deep in the Sweet Corn Field.

With this theory now in place,
one fear was all that stood;
If she strikes me out, I'll have
To run away for good.

Grandma stood and rubbed the ball,
She jacked the stitches high;
I swallowed hard, my hands were moist,
As she let the first one fly.

Thank you Lord, my whispered prayer
had found it's way above;
For the first pitch from my Grandma,
barely left her cow-hide glove.

A sigh of relief had found its way to
calm my beating heart;
I thought it might be over, As my
Grandpa fell apart.

"Struck me out three times you say,"
He laughed 'til he was blue;
"Ohhhh, piddle," snorted Grandma,
as she geared up for pitch two.

She wasn't going to give up now,
my Grandpa made her curse;
Under her breath, I dare not share,
Her gnarly, bad-mouth verse.

I clinched the bat and dug back in,
awaiting her next pitch;
And as it floated through the zone,
I swung without a hitch.

Never, have I ever crushed a
frozen rope so hard;
The sound erupted with a blast,
and echoed through the yard.

Everything worked perfectly,
except for one small thing;
The ball it never found the corn,
BUT, it met the tire swing.

AUGUST MOON

You see, the ball it ricocheted
into the old elm tree;
After first careening off my
Grandma's knobby knee.

A bullet up the middle, then Grandma
hit the dirt;
After rounding the bases, I checked
if she'd been hurt.

"I'm all right," she murmured, her
dentures stained with grass;
Her glasses sailed about eight feet,
but, she handled it with class.

My Grandpa, he was howling,
He had never laughed so hard;
My Grandma, flipped like Charlie Brown,
outside in his backyard.

My Grandma hobbled to the porch,
and sat upon the swing;
I said that I was sorry, but she
didn't say a thing

Shawn Powell

She looked at me with curious
eyes, and said with out a grin;
I think I know now what I did,
Let's try that pitch again.

Just then my Father had arrived
and entered through the gate
My rescuer had finally come,
eleven minutes late.

Worried about my Grandma,
we helped her back inside;
Apologizing once again,
she slapped me on the side.

"Don't worry Son, I'll be okay,
Grandma's went through worse;
It's not as though, I'll have to start
the headlights on my hearse."

I left that eve, with a stinging heart,
my mind was not intact;
But still I managed to connect on one,
A homer, that's a fact!

AUGUST MOON

That night I went to Grandma's
house, and checked up on her knee;
With a bag of ice, wrapped on tight,
She sipped upon her tea.

My grandpa, once the merry man,
Was now the acting nurse;
No longer was she swearing him,
She spoke without one curse.

I knelt beside my Grandma, as she
iced her swollen knee;
And I thought about the gestures,
she lovingly gave to me.

To show me how to throw her pitch,
to feed me for the game;
To take a sizzler off her knee,
Though Grandpa showed no shame.

And I'm thankful for the story,
for my life is so much richer;
To have known the "Queen of Drop Balls"
was My Grandma, The Pitcher

For my Grandmother, Dorothy Fite

Shawn Powell

P.S.: For the record, I never ran the bases, but if I did, I would have definitely scored.

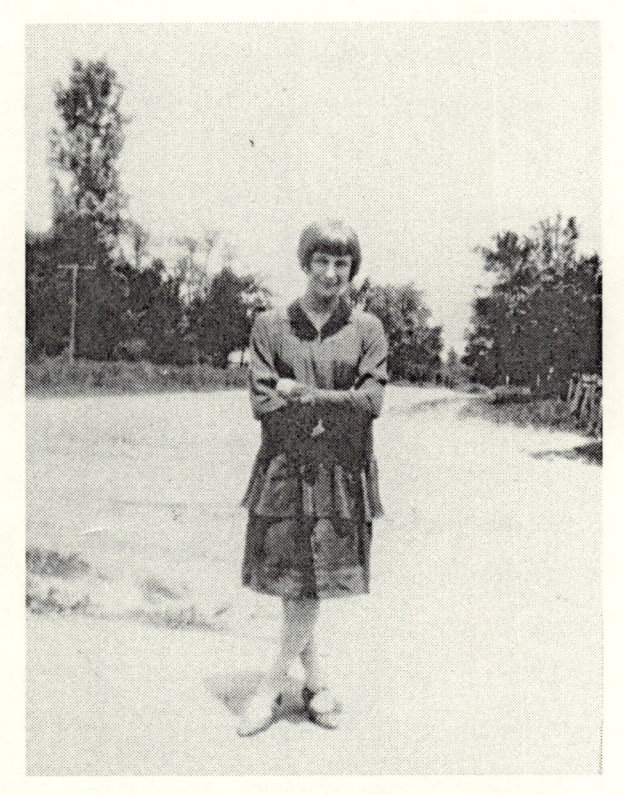

My Grandma the Pitcher, Dorothy Fite of Woodburn, Illinois

AUGUST MOON

STORY POEM IX

Shawn Powell

HEAVEN'S SKY

I sat inside an airplane,
as I flew one early morn;
Beside a woman, old in age,
her hands were rough and worn.

The sky, bright blue, I stared
in space, silence did I seek;
But next to me, I sensed a need;
the woman's need to speak.

I listened as her quips on life,
trembled with each word;
Her crippled hands held rosary beads;
My voice was seldom heard.

I sat and listened to her tales,
of the burdened life she gave;
Her bleeding heart was all that stood
before her sorrowed grave.

Shawn Powell

Her children are no longer here,
she lost them all to death;
Her husband lies in comatose,
He hangs on every breath.

I listened to her tired voice,
a sounding board was I;
A troubled soul whose end was near,
A tear fell from her eye.

And I thanked the Lord within my
seat, for all that he has done;
He blessed my home with health for all,
Both daughters and my son.

Compassion filled my aching soul,
as I gently grabbed her hand;
One tear was all that she had left,
I could not understand.

But as I flew through Heaven's sky,
God's message came quite clear;
An earthly Angel, she was blessed,
I saw Him, in her tear.

MY FAVORITE POEM

STUCK

By Alayna Powell
written at the age of 8 years

Once upon a time I saw
a small duck in a tree.
I asked him what he was doing,
And so he answered me:

You see, here I am,
And I don't know why,
But a silly old cat,
Led me up with his cry.

Oh that cat, he did trick me,
He told me he was stuck,
and after I got up here,
He laughed "Ha! Ha! Duck!"

So here I am
All out of luck,
Just sitting here
Stuck!